VINCENT VAN GOGH

Portrait of a Tortured Artist

THE HISTORY HOUR

CONTENTS

PART I
Introduction   1

PART II
EARLY LIFE
Christ of the Coal Mines   9

PART III
THE FIRST FOUR YEARS OF CREATIVITY
Domestic Life   15

PART IV
STYLISTIC DEVELOPMENTS AND INFLUENCES
The Academy of Fine Arts   27

PART V
PARIS
Cormon's Atelier   33

PART VI
ARLES
The Yellow House   43

PART VII
VAN GOGH AND GAUGUIN
The Event   53

PART VIII
Hospitalization   55

PART IX
LIFE IN AN ASYLUM
First Signs of Appreciation   65

PART X
Van Gogh's Death   67

PART XI
POSTHUMOUS FAME AND REPUTATION
Johanna Van Gogh-Bonger   79
The Van Gogh Museum   81

PART XII
Why Are van Gogh's Paintings So Valuable?   85

PART XIII
How Can We Use The Life of Van Gogh in Our
Own Lives?   89

PART XIV
Further Reading   91

Your Free eBook!   93

❦ I ❦
INTRODUCTION

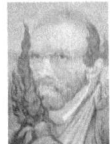

☙❦☙

Vincent Willem Van Gogh was born March 30, 1852, stillborn. Exactly one year later, Anna Cornelia Carbentus and Rev. Theodorus Van Gogh gave birth to a boy child whom they named Vincent Willem Van Gogh. The birth took place in Groot-Zundert, in the predominantly Catholic province of North Brabant in the southern Netherlands. This child grew into an adult and eventually became a painter who, although misunderstood in his lifetime, became recognized as one of the most important painters of his days and undoubtedly the most famous painter in the world during the twentieth century.

☙❦☙

Unlike most artists, Van Gogh developed very slowly, beginning with work as an art dealer that exposed him to many great works. He undertook this work for several years, after which he spent time as a missionary for the Dutch Reformed Church. Thereafter, he drifted for several years before returning home to his parents' house where he took up painting, largely self-taught with books on anatomy and painting. His great works all date from the later years of his life.

Wholly neglected in his life, he had psychosis for much of his life and was treated for depression, unsuccessfully. He died from a self-inflicted gun-shot wound on July 29th, 1890. Only after his death, thanks to the efforts of his brother, Theo, did he achieve recognition as a great artist.

❦ II ❦
EARLY LIFE

"I often think that the night is more alive and more richly colored than the day."

— VINCENT VAN GOGH

※

Vincent Van Gogh's father was a minister in the Dutch Reformed Church. Religion played an influential role in the young man's life, but art was a stronger draw for him. Three of Van Gogh's uncles on his father's side became art dealers. The Van Gogh family was largely made up of Dutch Reformed Ministers, but the Carbentus side of the family was affluent and influential in The Hague. Anna, Vincent's mother, was very religious and quite strict in her dedication to her family. She made efforts to keep others away from the family and schooled her children herself with the help of a governess until he was about six years old when he attended the village school at Zevenbergen. He befriended no one and was so miserable that he begged his parents to let him come home. Instead, they sent him to the middle school that was located in the royal palace in Tilburg where again he was deeply unhappy.

※

He had always been an exceptionally serious child, and at Tilburg, he became interested in art, as taught by the excellent art teacher who had had some success in Paris, Constant Cornelis Huijsmans. Huijsmans was the first Dutch art teacher and was extremely influential in The Netherlands as a teacher. He had a philosophy of art that stuck with young Vincent: he advocated abandoning technique in favor of capturing the impressions of objects and landscapes. This had been developed from his early exposure to the French artists of the pre-Impressionist movement. The other subjects that he excelled at included languages, where he was a top student. In 1868 though, he left school and never returned.

※

At age 16, Van Gogh's uncle (also named Vincent, and called '***Cent***') secured him a position as an apprentice art dealer for the Goupil & Company in The Hague. He completed his training by 1873 and was transferred to Goupil's London England branch at Southampton Street in London. He took lodgings at 87 Hackford Road, in Stockwell. He appeared to be happy at this time, and he was demonstrably good at his job, earning more money than his father.

※

His brother Theo also began working for Goupil & Company that year, and Theo was transferred to Brussels. The two brothers thus began a correspondence that would last for the rest of their lives. He fell in love with Eugénie Loyer, his landlady's daughter, but was rejected after he told her of his feelings and she responded that she was secretly engaged to a former lodger. This was a blow to Vincent, and he reacted by retreating into his religious faith.

❦

Van Gogh worked for Goupil in London from 1873 to May 1875. Daily contact with works of art from visits to the National Gallery in London and the British Museum developed his interest and knowledge of art, and he soon developed a fondness for Rembrandt van Rijn (1606-1669), Frans Hals (1582-1666), Johannes Vermeer (1632-75), and other Dutch masters. After learning of Vincent's social isolation, his father and his uncle Cent arranged for Vincent to be transferred to Paris in 1875. Here he was exposed to a very lucrative art market; his reaction to this was to grow bitter about the commodification of art as practiced by his company. A year later, when he made this feeling clear to the management, he was dismissed. In a letter to his brother Theo, he outlines his ambivalence to the position:

> *"...something has happened that didn't come as a total surprise to me. When I saw Mr. Boussod again, I asked if His Honor indeed thought it a good thing for me to go on working in the firm this year since His Honor never had any very serious complaints against me.*

❦

The latter was indeed the case, though, and His Honor took the words out of my mouth, so to speak, saying that I would leave on 1 April, thanking the gentlemen for anything I might have learned in their firm.

❧

When an apple is ripe, all it takes is a gentle breeze to make it fall from the tree; it's also like that here. I've certainly done things that were in some way very wrong, and so have little to say.

❧

And now, old boy, so far, I'm really rather in the dark about what I should do, but we must try and keep hope and courage alive."

❧

Despite his long and abiding hatred for the commodification of art, Van Gogh nevertheless developed a particular fondness for the works of French Romantic painters, particularly Jean-François Millet (1814-1875) and Jean Baptiste Camille Corot (1796-1875), whose influence was to last throughout his life. This picture, from 1857, called *The Gleaners*, is a particularly good example of Millet's work.

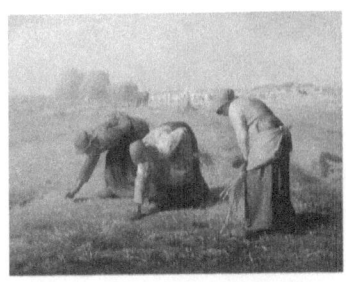

This painting by Camille Corot, called The Bridge at Narni, from 1826, is an excellent example of the pre-Impressionist style, maintaining precision and realism, a style that was so attractive to Van Gogh.

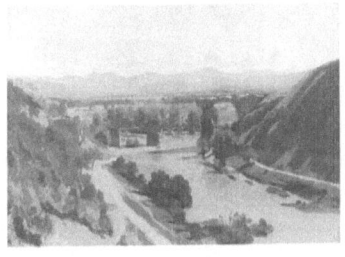

Always exceptionally adept at languages, Van Gogh returned to England in April of 1876 to work (unpaid) as a supply teacher for a boarding school in Ramsgate. Shortly thereafter, he moved to Middlesex with the proprietor of the school but did not stay. For the previous few years, Van Gogh was increasingly drawn to the Christian faith, peppering his letters to Theo more with Bible quotations and accounts of services and sermons than discussions of art. To this end, he took work as an assistant to a Methodist minister, which was also a short-term and unsatisfactory job for him. He later found a salaried position at a private school run by a vicar in Isleworth near London. He was allowed to preach at the school and in the surrounding villages, but the job offered very few prospects.

※

He decided to return to his parents' home. In the interim, they had moved to Etten, and by Christmas 1876, he was living in their house, working in a bookshop in Dordrecht, a job secured for him by his Uncle Cent. He was also unhappy here though, spending his days doodling and translating passages of the Bible into English, French, and German. He became increasingly pious and eschewed the ordinary joys of youth.

※

In 1877, his family arranged for him to move in with his uncle Johannes Stricker, a respected theologian, in Amsterdam. As a result of this, he began to prepare to enter the ministry, studying to qualify for the Theology school at the University of Amsterdam. He took the entrance exam, though, and failed it. The fact was, Vincent lacked the discipline necessary to study theology, preferring to walk around the city, observing nature. As a result of this, he decided to leave his uncle's house and took a three-month course to be a Protestant missionary at the school in Laken, near Brussels. He also failed in this course.

CHRIST OF THE COAL MINES

By January of 1879, Van Gogh accepted a post as a missionary at Petit-Wasmes in the coal-mining district called Borinage in modern-day Belgium. He described the congregation in a letter to Theo from April 1879:

> *"It's a somber place, and at first sight, everything around it has something dismal and deathly about it. The workers there are usually people, emaciated and pale owing to fever, who look exhausted and haggard, weather-beaten and prematurely old, the women generally sallow and withered."*

He was working with a very poor congregation and decided to give his lodgings at a bakery to a homeless person and moved into a small hut where he reportedly slept on straw, earning him the name **"*the Christ of the Coal Mines*."** Interestingly, the church was not pleased with this decision and dismissed him for "***undermining the dignity of the priesthood***" because of his slovenly appearance.

※

"They think I'm a madman,"

he told a friend,

> *"because I wanted to be a true Christian. They turned me out like a dog, saying that I was causing a scandal."*

Unemployed and hopeless, Van Gogh walked to Brussels, a journey of seventy-seven kilometers, returned to Cuesmes in Borinage, and finally returned to his parents' home in Etten. He remained living with his parents until March 1880, causing grief to his family, to such an extent that his father expressed the belief that he should be committed to the lunatic asylum at Geel.

III
THE FIRST FOUR YEARS OF CREATIVITY

"Great things are done by a series of small things brought together."

— VINCENT VAN GOGH

Van Gogh returned to Cuesmes in August 1880, where he lodged with a miner until October. According to letters to his brother Theo, he became interested in the people around him and began to draw them. Using these works, he applied to study with the Dutch artist Willem Roelofs, who was sufficiently impressed with him to urge him to apply to the Académie Royale des Beaux-Arts in Brussels. He registered at the Académie in November 1880 and studied anatomy and the standard rules of modeling and perspective.

In April 1881, Vincent returned to live with his parents in Etten for an extended stay. He continued to draw and sketch, perfecting his style and used his neighbors as his subjects.

"I want to give the wretched a brotherly message,"

he explained to Theo.

"When I sign them 'Vincent,' it is as one of them."

At some level, Theo managed to convince Vincent that he would be better serving God as an artist than as a minister.

During this time, in August of 1881, a recently widowed cousin and a family friend came to visit from Amsterdam with her eight-year-old son. Van Gogh, who, as a rule, did not take kindly to strangers, began courting her, taking long walks with Cornelia "***Kee***" Vos-Stricker. To almost everyone's surprise and to her dismay, he declared his love and proposed marriage, to which she famously answered (in Dutch)

"nooit, neen, nimmer,"

which translates roughly to

"no, nay, never!"

Obviously, Van Gogh was devastated.

Shortly thereafter, Van Gogh traveled to The Hague to try to sell some of his paintings and to meet with the successful painter, and his second cousin, Anton Mauve (1838-88). Mauve and he apparently got along well, as Mauve invited him to return in a few months, suggesting he spend the intervening time drawing exclusively with charcoal. Vincent returned to Etten to follow this suggestion.

※

Late in November 1881, Vincent wrote an angry letter to the theologian Johannes Stricker (1816-86) concerning his love for Stricker's daughter Kee, and shortly after that, he left for Amsterdam. Cornelia ("**Kee**") Vos-Stricker continued to refuse even to meet him in Amsterdam. In despair, he held his left hand in the flame of a lamp, saying:

> *"Let me see her for as long as I can keep my hand in the flame."*

He did not recall the incident but later assumed that his uncle had blown out the flame. Cornelia's father Johannes made it clear that her refusal was final and that they would never marry mainly because he was no longer able to support himself.

※

Anton Mauve did agree to take Van Gogh as a student though and introduced him to the art of watercolor painting. He worked on for the next month before returning home for Christmas. He did not get along with his father, refused to attend church, and left for The Hague shortly afterward. Within a month, Van Gogh and Mauve fell out, and Vincent could afford to hire only people from the street as models, a practice that Mauve disapproved of, because of the company Van Gogh was keeping.

In June, Van Gogh suffered a bout of gonorrhea and spent nearly a month in the hospital. Soon after, he bought his first oil paints with money he borrowed from his younger brother and protector, Theo, and tried his hand at oil painting. He liked the medium and spread the paint liberally, scraping from the canvas and working back with the brush. He wrote that he was surprised at how good the results were. Even from this earliest period, Van Gogh used oil paint both as a color and as a contour, giving his work an almost three-dimensional look, making his oils very thick and taking a long time to dry.

DOMESTIC LIFE

※

By March 1882, Mauve expressed his disappointment with Van Gogh and stopped replying to his letters. He seems to have learned that Van Gogh was living with a woman described in much of the literature as an alcoholic former prostitute, named Clasina Maria "**Sien**" Hoornik (1850–1904), and her young daughter. Although these hyperbolic and vitriolic attacks against the woman who became Van Gogh's only domestic relationship persist through the literature, there is no evidence that she was anything more than a seamstress, cleaning woman, and mother. She was Van Gogh's model as well, and the work he did with her was some of the grittiest and most honest work he ever achieved.

※

Vincent had met Sien towards the end of January 1882 and used her as a drawing Sorrow. At the time, she had a five-year-old daughter and was pregnant with another child.

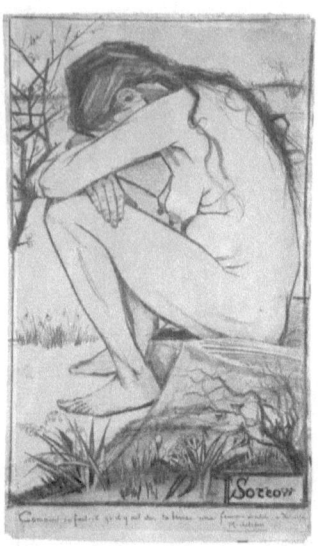

In June 1882, Van Gogh was hospitalized for a bout of gonorrhea. Disobeying doctor's orders, he left the hospital July 1 to visit Sien Hoornik in Leiden, where she had just given birth to a baby boy, whom they named Willem. Van Gogh moved to a larger studio next door with Sien and her two children. Hoornik was ill after the birth though and needed a period of recovery after a very difficult pregnancy and delivery. The baby boy, though, brought a great deal of happiness to Van Gogh. In Van Gogh's mind, this would help him to reach deeper into his artistic sensibility and his sensibilities as a man.

Sien Hoornik had previously borne two children who had died, but Van Gogh did not know about this, and when Van

Gogh's father found out that he had had an illegitimate child with a "***prostitute***," he strongly advised Van Gogh to leave her. Initially, Van Gogh refused and considered moving with his new family away from the city, but later in the year, he bowed to pressure from his brother, Theo, and left her and the children. Vincent described and defended his relationship in a contemporary letter to Theo:

> *"People suspect me of something... it's in the air... I must be hiding something... Vincent is keeping something back that may not be divulged. Well, gentlemen, I'll tell you, you who set great store by manners and culture, and rightly so, provided it's the real thing, what is more cultured, more sensitive, more manly: to forsake a woman or to take on a forsaken one?"*

※

The family life of his new home became unbearable to a man with such sensitivities though and, after Van Gogh left, Sien Hoornik returned to her working life again. The tragic breaking up of this little family is a testament to the prudishness of the religious family and their propensity to do the opposite of what their spiritual leader asked of them, but nevertheless, Sien Hoornik was forced to give up her daughter to her mother and baby Willem to her brother. Willem believed Van Gogh was his father, but the timing of his birth makes this unlikely. Van Gogh and Sien never reconciled, and she drowned herself in the River Scheldt in 1904.

※

In September 1883, Van Gogh moved to Drenthe in the

northern Netherlands. This was an isolated part of the country frequented by artists including Mauve, and he stayed there for three productive months. In December, driven by intense loneliness, he went back to live with his parents at their new home in Nuenen, in northern Brabant. Here, he continued to paint still life figures and landscapes, all influenced by and attempting to depict the life of the peasants who surrounded him.

※

Van Gogh was always very strongly inclined toward the plight of the poor and the destitute, and when French novelist Emile Zola published his novel, Germinal, in 1885, Van Gogh read it and was strongly affected by the sociological depth, trying to depict this in such works as The Potato Eaters and The Weavers, (see page following) which he painted during these years.

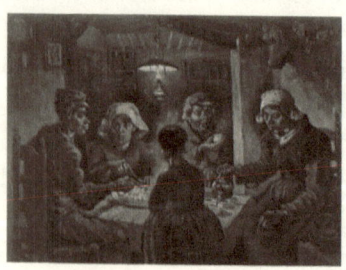

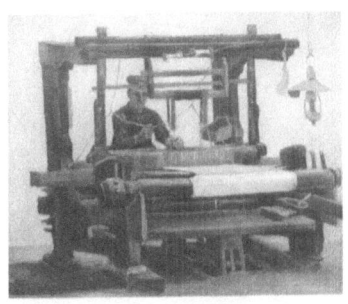

Theo had been sending him money for several years by this point, and finally, Vincent tried to repay him. In a letter from 1884, he proposed to send his works to Theo in exchange for the allowance:

> *"Now I have a proposal to make for the future. Let me send you my work, and you take what you want from it, but I insist that I may consider the money I would receive from you after March as money I've earned."*

༺☙༻

Of course, Vincent hoped that Theo would be able to sell his paintings, but they were not of the fashionable Impressionist style, drab in color and deep in psychological angst. Consequently, Theo had great trouble selling any of them and failed miserably.

IV
STYLISTIC DEVELOPMENTS AND INFLUENCES

"There may be a great fire in our hearts, yet no one ever comes to warm himself at it, and the passers-by see only a wisp of smoke."

— VINCENT VAN GOGH

Van Gogh increasingly understood the possibilities in his paintings during these years, by studying the work of painters like the Flemish master Frans Hals (1582-1666), who taught him the way to depict the freshness of visual impressions. Similarly, his studies of the Venetian Renaissance painter Paolo Veronese (1528-88) and the French Romantic painter Eugène Delacroix (1798-1863) taught him a great deal about the importance of using color to express an idea by itself.

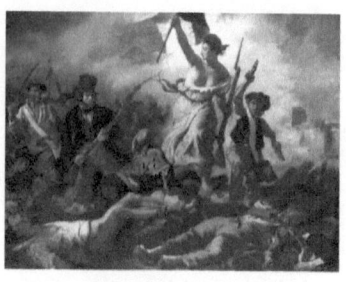

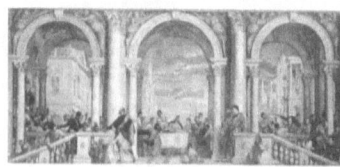

He had been long interested in the work of Peter Paul Rubens (1577-1640) as well and suddenly decided to set out for Antwerp where the largest collection of Rubens' work was to be found. The revelation of Rubens' mode of direct notation and of his ability to express a mood through a combination of colors proved decisive in the development of Van Gogh's style. This can be seen in the following painting, The Fall of Phaeton.

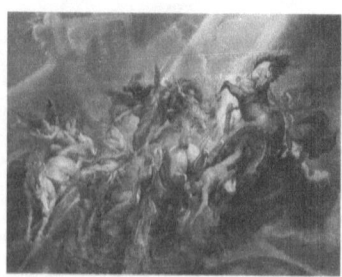

Simultaneously, Van Gogh discovered two very different kinds of art: Japanese prints and Impressionist painting. All these sources influenced him more than the academic principles taught at the Antwerp Academy, where he had enrolled. He refused to follow the academy's dictates which led to disputes, and after three months, he left the school in 1886 to join Theo in Paris.

※

In Paris, Van Gogh met Henri de Toulouse-Lautrec (1864-1901), who was to be so closely associated with the Parisian demimonde, particularly at the Moulin Rouge, and who drew a portrait of Van Gogh.

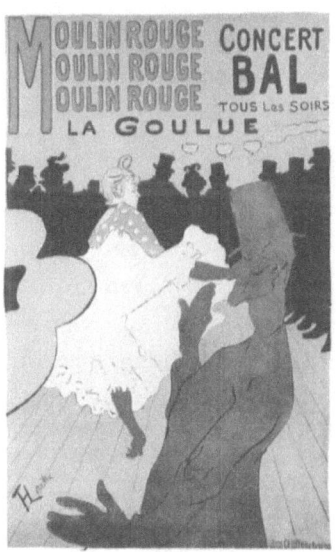

Paul Gauguin (1848-1903), who later moved to Tahiti, was to play an important role in Van Gogh's development. These artists opened Van Gogh's mind to the latest developments in French painting.

※

He also met with some of the Impressionists like Camille Pissarro (1830-1903), Georges Seurat (1859-1901), and others.

※

In 1883, Van Gogh moved to Nuenen where he focused on painting and drawing. Working outside and extremely quickly, he completed sketches and paintings of weavers and their cottages.

※

Beginning in August 1884, Margot Begemann, a neighbor's daughter ten years older than him, joined him on his visits to the local peasants. She fell in love with him, and they decided to marry, but neither side of their families was in favor. Margot was devastated and took an overdose of strychnine but survived when Van Gogh rushed her to a nearby hospital. On 26 March 1885, though, tragedy struck Van Gogh again when his father died of a heart attack. Shortly thereafter, he realized that he was an embarrassment to his family and moved out of the family home into his studio.

※

In 1885, Van Gogh painted several groups of still lives. During his two-year stay in Nuenen, he completed many drawings and watercolors and nearly two hundred oil paintings. His palette consisted mainly of somber earth tones, particularly dark brown, with none of the vivid colors of his mature style.

※

For the first time, there was some interest in his work from a dealer in Paris early in 1885. Theo asked Vincent if he had paintings ready to exhibit and in May, Van Gogh responded with his first major work, The Potato Eaters, and a series of ***"peasant character studies"*** which were the culmination of several years of work. When he complained that Theo was not making enough effort to sell his paintings in Paris, his brother told him that they were too dark and brooding, and not in keeping with the new bright style of Impressionism. In August, his work was publicly exhibited for the first time, in the shop windows of the dealer called Leurs in The Hague. When one of his young peasant sitters became pregnant in September 1885, however, Van Gogh was accused of forcing himself upon her, and thereafter the village priest forbade his parishioners from modeling for him. Whether this incident is true or not is the subject of much study and conjecture but was never verified.

※

In November of 1885, though, bowing to the pressure from the community, Van Gogh moved to Antwerp, renting a small room above a paint dealer's shop in the Lange Beeldekensstraat. He never returned to the Netherlands again. In Antwerp, he lived in great poverty and ate poorly, supported almost entirely by money sent by his brother Theo. He spent the money sent to him on painting materials and models. Bread, coffee, and tobacco became his staple diet, and as a result, severe malnutrition was a constant worry.

His teeth became loose and painful to him, and, in February 1886, he wrote in a letter to his brother that he had only had six hot meals since the previous May.

※

In Antwerp, he applied himself to the study of color theory and spent a great deal of time in museums studying the work of Rubens. With the information he got from these studies, he managed to do what Theo had asked, broadening his palette to include colors like carmine, cobalt blue, and emerald green. Van Gogh also bought Japanese ukiyo-e (literally "***pictures of the floating world***") woodcuts from sailors who had returned from Japan, incorporating elements of this style into the background of some of his paintings, and decorating the walls of his studio with them.

※

He had always been a heavy drinker, and this weakness was becoming more pronounced during this time. In fact, he admitted himself to hospital between February and March of 1886. It is suspected that he was suffering from syphilis.

THE ACADEMY OF FINE ARTS

❧

When he recovered from this illness, he decided to apply to formal study and took the higher-level admission tests at the Academy of Fine Arts in Antwerp, graduating in January 1886, with a specialization in painting and drawing. As a result of his dangerous and self-destructive lifestyle which including heavy drinking and smoking, he became increasingly rundown.

❧

Vincent wrote to his brother Theo about his experiences in the Academy:

> *"I actually find all the drawings I see there hopelessly bad and fundamentally wrong. And I know that mine are totally different, time will just have to tell who's right. Damn it, not one of them has any feeling for what a classical statue is."*

In January 1886, shortly after graduating, he began to attend classes in drawing after plaster models but ran into trouble with the director of the Academy, Charles Veriat because of his strange painting style. He was also at odds with the instructor, Franz Vinck, and switched into the class offered by Eugène Siberdt, a class in painting after antique plaster models. He ran into conflict with Siberdt as well though because the class required to express the contour of the model and the lines. For example, rather than reproducing the Venus de Milo statue, he produced a naked and limbless peasant woman. Although Van Gogh was not intentionally defying Siberdt, Siberdt regarded this as a kind of defiance against his artistic guidance and made corrections to Van Gogh's drawing with his crayon so violently that he actually tore the paper. Van Gogh was furious and, according to the reports from his fellow students, began shouting at Siberdt:

> *"you clearly do not know what a young woman is like, God damn it! A woman must have hips, buttocks, a pelvis in which she can carry a baby!"*

This was likely the last time he attended the class. Shortly after this, the teachers of the Academy decided that he would have to repeat the year, but Van Gogh decided instead to leave the school.

❧ V ☙
PARIS

"The fishermen know that the sea is dangerous and the storm terrible, but they have never found these dangers sufficient reason for remaining ashore."

— VINCENT VAN GOGH

☙❦☙

Van Gogh moved to Paris shortly afterward unannounced, arriving on February 28th, just before a letter explaining his decision arrived at Theo's apartment.

"My dear Theo,

> *Don't be cross with me that I've come all of a sudden. I've thought about it so much, and I think we'll save time this way. Will be at the Louvre from midday, or earlier if you like. A reply, please, to*

let me know when you could come to the Salle Carrée. As for expenses, I repeat, it comes to the same thing. I have some money left that goes without saying, and I want to talk to you before spending anything. We'll sort things out, you'll see. So, get there as soon as possible. I shake your hand."

In Paris, he shared the apartment in the rue Laval in Montmartre with his brother Theo. He applied and was accepted to Fernand Cormon's studio. In June, Theo finally found and rented a larger flat in 54 rue Lepic.

Van Gogh had renewed vigor now, thanks to a better diet and new scenery and people to paint. This was reflected in his style, with his color palette increasingly broad and lighter. He produced many portraits of his friends and acquaintances and the famous series of paintings of the Moulin de la Galette. Also, he created scenes of life in Montmartre, Asnières, and of people walking along the Seine River. He continued collecting the Japanese ukiyo-e woodcuts and began to try to emulate them when he traced a figure from a reproduction of a painting by Keisai Eisen on the cover of the Paris Illustré magazine. He entitled this work The Courtesan or Oiran (1887), and then graphically enlarged it into an oil painting.

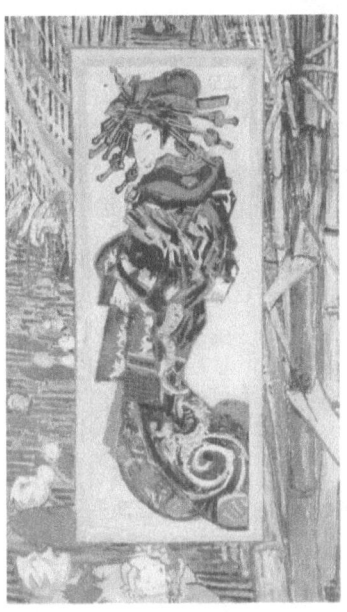

After seeing the self-portrait by the French painter Adolphe Monticelli (1824-86) at the Galerie Delareybarette, Van Gogh resolved to adopt his brighter palette and his bold attack, particularly in paintings such as his Seascape near Saintes-Maries (1888, see next page). The brighter colors made his work much more joyous, and his new style of painting with very short brush strokes gave it a contemporary feel. Van Gogh was so taken with the style of Monticelli that two years later, he and his brother Theo paid for the publication of a book on Monticelli paintings, and Vincent bought some of Monticelli's works to add to his collection.

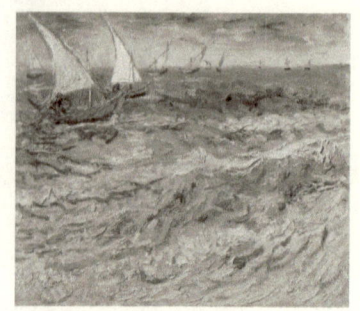

CORMON'S ATELIER

❧

Van Gogh worked at Fernand Cormon's atelier throughout April and May of 1886, where he became close with members of the circle of the Australian artist John Peter Russell (1858-1930), who painted his portrait in 1886. Van Gogh also met Émile Bernard, Louis Anquetin and Henri de Toulouse-Lautrec – who painted a portrait of him in pastel.

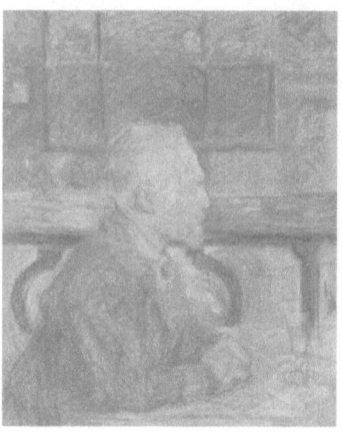

They met at the famous paint shop owned by Julien "***Père***" Tanguy, (which was, at that time, the only place where anyone could see the paintings of Paul Cézanne, the great Impressionist.) In that year, two large exhibitions were mounted there, showing the new styles of Pointillism and Neo-impressionism for the first time, and bringing the work of Georges Seurat and Paul Signac into the public consciousness. Theo kept some Impressionist paintings in his gallery on Boulevard Montmartre, and so Van Gogh was already familiar with this style, but he had a difficult time accepting this style as something important.

༺✦༻

Naturally, with a living arrangement like theirs, there arose conflicts between the two brothers. Theo was a very well organized and successful businessman in the field of art, and Vincent was very disillusioned with the art market and what he perceived as commodification of something that was essentially priceless. Nevertheless, Theo supported Vincent despite reporting to friends that life with Vincent was "***almost unbearable***." By early 1887, they were again at peace, and Vincent had moved to Asnières, a northwestern suburb of Paris, where he got to know Signac quite well. He adopted elements of Pointillism, a technique in which a multitude of small colored dots is applied to the canvas so that when seen from a distance, they create an optical blend of hues. The style stresses the power of complementary colors to form vibrant contrasts. While living in Asnières, Van Gogh painted the local parks and restaurants and created some amazing scenes of life on the Seine, including Bridges across the Seine at Asnières, in a style reminiscent (but not exactly like) Seurat.

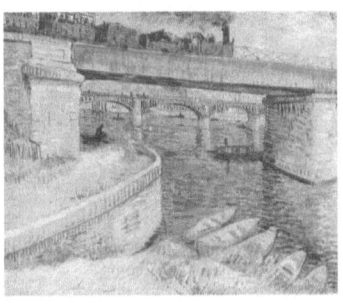

Before these terrible life drama events occurred, though, Van Gogh was very prolific in his painting, creating nearly two hundred paintings while he lived in Paris, a stay that lasted only about two years.

※

In December 1887, Van Gogh organized an exhibition alongside Émile Bernard, Louis Anquetin, and Toulouse-Lautrec at the Grand-Bouillon Restaurant du Chalet, 43 Avenue de Clichy in Montmartre. Bernard claimed that it was received with awe and that it was far ahead of anything Parisians had ever seen. Bernard and Anquetin had success selling their first paintings, but Van Gogh did not. He did, however, exchange some paintings with Gauguin.

※

This exhibition engendered numerous discussions on art, artists, and their place in society. According to reports, it included artists like Camille Pissarro, his son Lucien Pissarro, Paul Signac and Georges Seurat. In February 1888, he paid his first and only visit to Seurat at his studio. Although this visit was a success, Van Gogh left for Arles the next day, thoroughly burnt out by his Parisian lifestyle.

※

As he wrote to his brother, Theo, he found living in Paris inspiring for ideas but exceedingly difficult to work:

> *"It seems to me almost impossible to be able to work in Paris unless you have a refuge in which to recover and regain your peace of mind and self-composure. Without that, you'd be bound to get utterly numbed."*

VI
ARLES

"I dream of painting and then I paint my dream."

— VINCENT VAN GOGH

※

While living in Paris, Van Gogh was introduced to the popular and highly intoxicating drink called absinthe. Until it was banned, it was responsible for a remarkable number of people going mad and doing things that they would never normally do. But this drink that he favored so much was responsible at least in part for his declining health in Paris, and thus he decided to move to Arles, in Provence in southwest France, in February 1888.

※

According to his correspondence with Theo, he had a dream to form an artist's colony there. He rented the eastern wing of a house he called the Yellow House, located at 2 places Lamartine for fifteen francs per month. This wing had not been inhabited for many years and had fallen into disrepair and was unfurnished. He had thought he would be able to move right in but was disappointed when he arrived to find its state. Taking a train trip that lasted a day and a night, he finally arrived on February 20th, 1888 in Arles, a small town on the River Rhône.

He moved first into the Hôtel Carrel, and then on 7 May, to the Café de la Gare at the invitation of its proprietors, Joseph and Marie Ginoux, who had become his good friends, and Marie would later become the subject of his series of L'Arlesienne portraits.

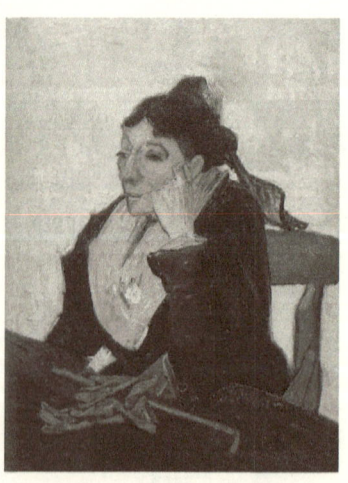

He invited the Danish painter Christian Mourier-Petersen (1858-1945) to join him in Arles, and he stayed for two months, recalling later that Arles seemed like a foreign country, in comparison to Paris:

> *"The Zouaves [the Algerian soldiers stationed in the town], the brothels, the adorable little Arlésienne going to her First Communion, the priest in his surplice, who looks like a dangerous rhinoceros, the people drinking absinthe, all seem, to me, creatures from another world."*

※

While living in Arles, Van Gogh completed two hundred oil paintings and more than one hundred drawings and watercolors. He was inspired by the local landscape and the unique light of the southern French landscape, including rich yellows, ultramarine, and mauve. He even took a trip to the seashore, several hours away, to paint the sea and the boats. These colors are strongly inspired by the work of renaissance Italian artists like Veronese, who prized gold and ultramarine more than any other colors. To incorporate these colors into his palette, he painted harvests and other rural events, which were rich in the yellows, including The Old Mill (1888), a picturesque structure bordering the wheat fields. This and six other paintings were sent in October 1888 as an exchange with Paul Gauguin, Émile Bernard, and Charles Laval.

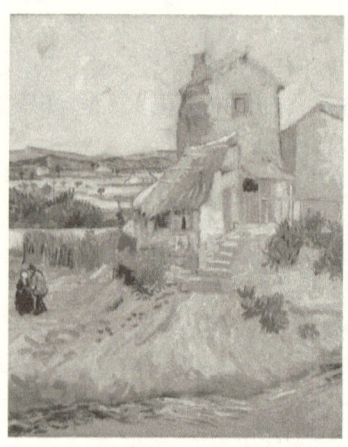

One of the techniques Van Gogh employed in his Arles landscapes is a gridded perspective frame, which was a frame suspended above the ground to give the painter a sense of what he would capture in the final project. Below is a sketch, done by Van Gogh, of the frame and of himself using it (or, more accurately, how he thought he would use it).

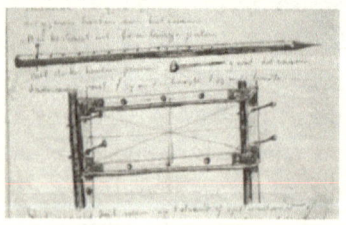

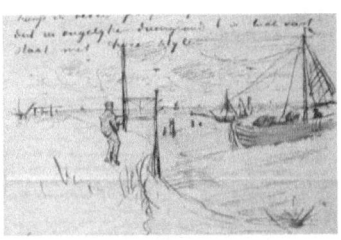

At this time, three of his Arlesian landscapes were shown at the annual exhibition of the Société des Artistes Indépendants in Paris. In April, he was visited by the American artist Dodge MacKnight (1860-1950) who was living nearby at Fontvieille.

THE YELLOW HOUSE

※

He used the Yellow House as a studio and slowly furnished it. Using it as a subject, he painted a series of paintings depicting the interior of this house and surrounding buildings and scenes, including Van Gogh's Chair (1888), Bedroom in Arles (1888), The Night Café (1888), Café Terrace at Night (September 1888), Starry Night Over the Rhone (1888), and Still Life: Vase with Twelve Sunflowers (1888), all to be used as decoration for the Yellow House.

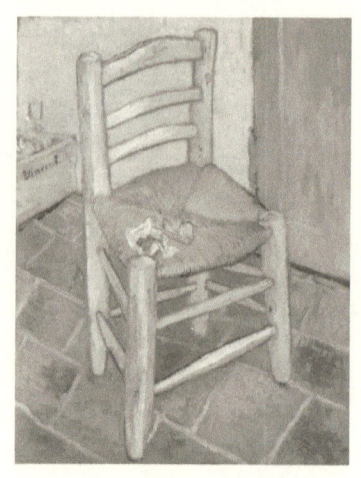

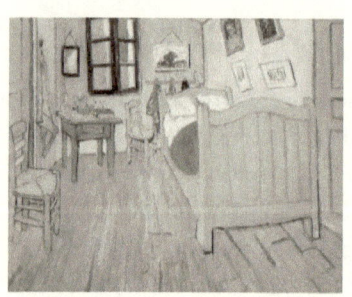

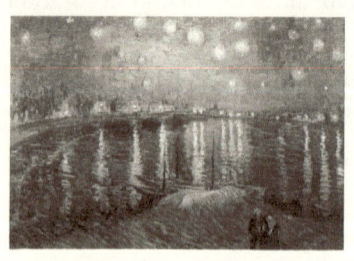

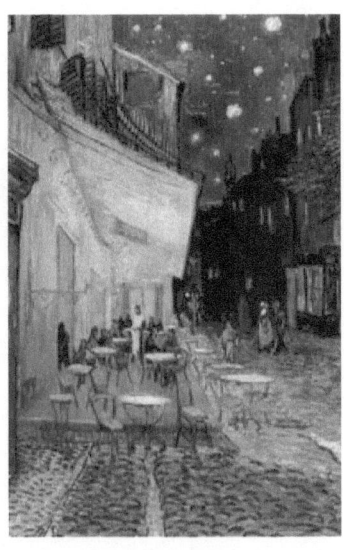

About The Night Café, Van Gogh wrote that he tried to express

> *"the idea that a café is a place where one can ruin oneself, go mad, or commit a crime."*

When he visited Saintes-Maries-de-la-Mer in June, he gave painting lessons to an Algerian Zouave second lieutenant named Paul-Eugène Milliet and painted boats on the sea and the village. MacKnight introduced Van Gogh to the Belgian painter Eugène Boch, who was staying in nearby Fontvieille, in July.

※

He received word that Paul Gauguin was planning to visit him at Arles in August of 1888, and while waiting for his arrival, Van Gogh painted his now famous Sunflowers. He also painted a portrait of Boch, and a study he called The Poet Against a Starry Sky.

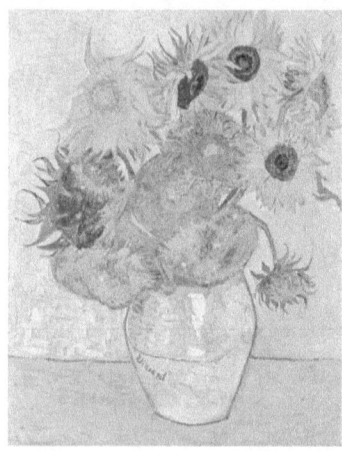

Slowly furnishing the Yellow House, Van Gogh bought two beds and then on September 17ty, 1888, he spent his first night in the Yellow House. He also began work on the large Décoration for the Yellow House, probably the most ambitious effort he ever undertook. This was a three-step series of paintings, beginning with his sunflower paintings, followed by a series of portraits, and finally, a series of landscapes of the surrounding area. He completed two chair paintings, Van Gogh's Chair and Gauguin's Armchair before Gauguin arrived.

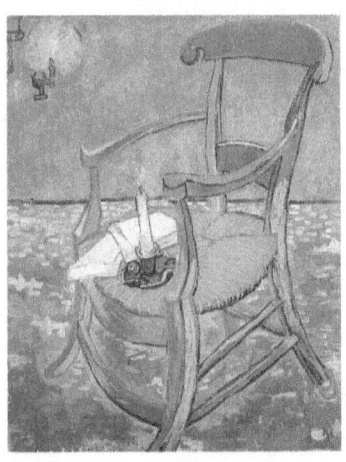

Gauguin was not totally convinced that his visit would be a good idea. He was well-aware that Van Gogh was unstable as a companion and vacillated between staying in Paris and going to stay with Van Gogh. After several pleading letters from Van Gogh, Gauguin finally arrived in Arles on October 23, and in November the two started painting together.

VII
VAN GOGH AND GAUGUIN

"There is no blue without yellow and without orange."

— VINCENT VAN GOGH

In November 1887, before he departed for Arles, Van Gogh attended an exhibition of post-Impressionist Paul Gauguin's Martinique paintings, which were being exhibited at the gallery of the color merchant Arsène Poitier's. Van Gogh visited with his brother, Theo, because of the connection between Goupil & Cie and Portier. In fact, Theo bought three of Gauguin's paintings for nine hundred francs and arranged to have them displayed at Goupil's, thus providing Gauguin with access to wealthy clients. At the same time, Van Gogh and Gauguin became close friends, and they frequently spoke about art. According to Gauguin, these conversations were the basis of his theory of art that he developed around this time. Van Gogh enjoyed these discussions but, according to a letter he wrote to his brother Theo,

> *"Gauguin and I talk a lot about Delacroix,*
> *Rembrandt &c. The discussion is excessively*
> *electric. We sometimes emerge from it with tired*
> *minds, like an electric battery after it's*
> *run down."*

Despite the fruitful conversations, Gauguin and Van Gogh did not get along particularly well. Their relationship was not an equal one though; Gauguin felt that Van Gogh was at a more rudimentary level in his skill and tended to be arrogant about his own abilities while Van Gogh wanted to be treated as an equal despite the adulation he felt for Gauguin. Gauguin painted Van Gogh in The Painter of Sunflowers and encouraged him to develop his skills of painting from memory. This was a skill that Van Gogh took to with great energy and which served him for the rest of his life.

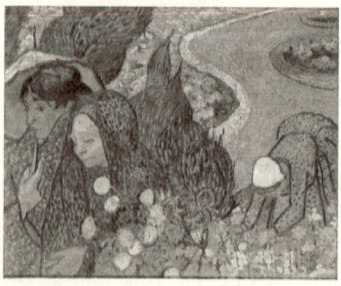

Van Gogh painted Memory of the Garden at Etten is one such painting he did from memory, and the two painters joined together to create the pendants called Les Alyscamps. Van Gogh created two autumn scenes in the ancient Roman necropolis, and Gauguin created his own version, which he completed after he left Arles. Gauguin, for his part, only completed one painting, Van Gogh Painting Sunflowers, while staying with Van Gogh. This was because the relationship they had was unhealthy and caused both of them a great deal of grief.

❃

Van Gogh was notoriously hard to get along with, and when Van Gogh invited Gauguin to join him at his Yellow House in Arles, they began to quarrel, and Gauguin decided to leave. It appears that Van Gogh was drinking a great deal at this time and that the weather was inclement, forcing the two painters to remain indoors at a time in their relationship when they were not getting along well. Gauguin was domineering, according to Van Gogh, and Gauguin suspected that he was being exploited by the two Van Gogh brothers (Vincent, to increase his reputation which was less than Gauguin's, and Theo, because he owed him money for some paintings that he had sold).

THE EVENT

༺༻

For several days, Vincent Van Gogh was behaving oddly, and on the day of the event, December 23rd, 1888, Gauguin had gone out for a walk, followed by Van Gogh, holding a razor. They had an altercation which ended inconclusively, and Van Gogh returned to his own room in the Yellow House. According to his account, he was hearing voices that urged him to cut off his own ear with the razor. It caused severe bleeding, and so he bandaged his ear, around his head (as the painting of this shows). In a particularly gruesome gesture, he then took his ear, wrapped it in a newspaper, and handed it to a woman named Rachel who worked at a brothel that the two painters had visited; he asked her to

"keep this object carefully, in remembrance of me."

༺༻

The next day, a policeman found Van Gogh and took him to the hospital. Gauguin left Arles, never to see Van Gogh again, although they continued to write to one another for several years. In fact, in 1890, Gauguin proposed that he and Van Gogh form an artist's studio in Antwerp. Gauguin's 1889 Jug in the Form of a Head, featuring red dribbles coming from a nonexistent ear, seems to bear witness to this bizarre event with Van Gogh.

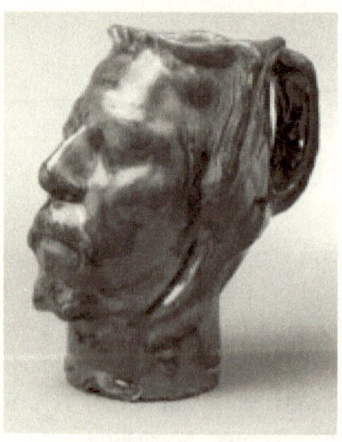

❦ VIII ❧
HOSPITALIZATION

"What would life be if we had no courage to attempt anything?"

— VINCENT VAN GOGH

❦

At the hospital, he was treated by a young doctor in training named Félix Rey. The ear was brought to the hospital, but Rey did not try to reattach it as too much time had passed, and the piece was no longer living.

❦

Van Gogh seems to have had no memory of the event and believed that he had had an acute mental breakdown. Dr. Rey attributed his behavior as "***acute mania with generalized***

delirium," and because of this, as well as the report of the policeman who had found him, he was put into hospital care. Gauguin notified Theo of the situation, and Theo rushed to be with his brother, even though he had just proposed to Johanna Bonger. He arrived on Christmas Day and tried his best to comfort Vincent, who was only semiconscious. Theo returned to Paris the next day with Gauguin. Later, he wrote to his fiancée that:

> *"I found Vincent in the hospital in Arles. The people around him realized from his agitation that for the past few days he had been showing symptoms of that most dreadful illness, of madness, and an attack of "**fièvre chaude**," when he injured himself with a knife, was the reason he was taken to the hospital. Will he remain insane? The doctors think it possible but daren't yet say for certain."*

☙❧

The doctors did not believe that Van Gogh would recover from his psychotic episode, but nevertheless, Van Gogh left the hospital on January 7, 1889. He returned for treatment to the hospital, living in the Yellow House. This horrific event made the local newspapers and horrified the local citizens, who petitioned the town to close the Yellow House rented by "***le fou roux***" (the "***crazy ginger***") in March.

☙❧

Van Gogh, who seems to have been poisoned by a habit he had of drinking turpentine, was suffering from hallucinations and delusions. As strange as this sounds, it is a common thing for painters to drink small amounts of turpentine, and it is in fact identified as an addictive substance, which causes build-up in the body that amounts to poison over time.

⁂

In April 1889, Van Gogh had befriended the doctor who treated him to such a degree that he moved in with him after his own quarters, and some of his paintings were damaged by floods. Before he left, Van Gogh gave a gift of a portrait to Dr. Rey, and Dr. Rey apparently was not fond of the work and used it to repair a chicken coop, and then gave it away for free. It is now at the Pushkin Museum and valued at upwards of fifty million dollars. He stayed in Arles for two more months and voluntarily entered the Saint-Paul-de-Mausole Asylum in Saint-Rémy-de-Provence.

❦ IX ❦
LIFE IN AN ASYLUM

"I feel that there is nothing more truly artistic than to love people."

— VINCENT VAN GOGH

※

Van Gogh entered the Saint-Paul-de-Mausole asylum accompanied by Frédéric Salles, a Protestant clergyman, on May 8, 1889. Saint-Paul-de-Mausole is a Romanesque building that used to be a monastery in Saint-Rémy, located close to Arles, and was run by a former naval doctor named Théophile Peyron. It was not a typical nineteenth-century lunatic asylum, and Van Gogh was given two cells with barred windows, one of which was he used as a painting studio. The regimented lifestyle, very different from Van Gogh's normal life, gave him certain stability with which to resume his work. He wrote:

> *"I feel happier here with my work than I could be outside. By staying here, a good long time, I shall have learned regular habits, and in the long run, the result will be more order in my life."*

Nevertheless, there does not seem to have been much in the way of actual treatment for his illness, other than denial of coffee, alcohol, and other intoxicants, including turpentine oil. He received two two-hour baths per week, which seem to have had some benefit. The food was terrible, according to his account, consisting mainly of bread and soup.

※

He had limits to his inspiration at the clinic though, despite the beauty of the Romanesque architecture. The clinic and its garden were his main subjects. He made studies of the hospital's interior, including Vestibule of the Asylum and Saint-Rémy which he completed in September 1889, and some of his works are characterized by swirls, such as in his famous The Starry Night. He was allowed short supervised walks, when he painted cypresses and olive trees, including Olive Trees with the Alpilles in the Background 1889, Cypresses 1889, Cornfield with Cypresses (1889), and Country Road in Provence by Night (1890). In September 1889, he produced two other versions of his Bedroom in Arles painting.

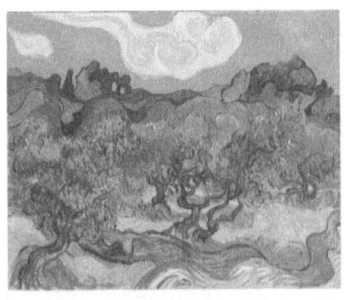

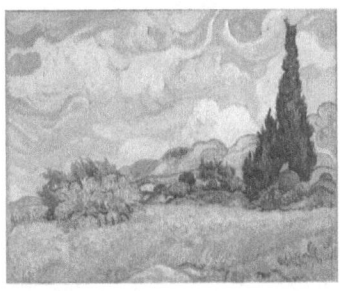

Theo married Johanna Bonger in Amsterdam in April 1889. In January 1890, Van Gogh received a birth announcement in the mail at Saint-Rémy. Theo and Johanna had named their son after him: Vincent Willem Van Gogh. After the birth of his nephew, Van Gogh wrote:

> *"I'd much rather that he'd called his boy after Pa, whom I've thought about so often these days, than after me, but anyway, as it's been done now, I started right away to make a picture for him, to hang in their bedroom, branches of white almond blossom against a blue sky."*

Vincent sent them the painting from the hospital intended for the young boy entitled Almond Blossom.

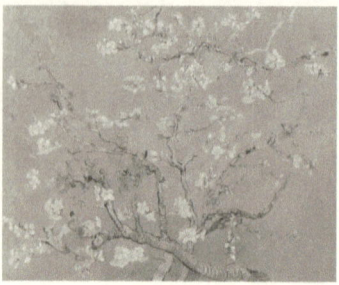

To aid in his recovery, Van Gogh wrote to his brother and his mother, asking them to send him his earlier work so that he could use them as inspiration for new work, and to complete his earlier unfinished pieces. Some of the works from this period, which many critics consider his mature work, and some of his best work includes Sorrowing Old Man ("*At Eternity's Gate*"), described as "*another unmistakable remembrance of times long past*." His late paintings show an artist at the height of his abilities.

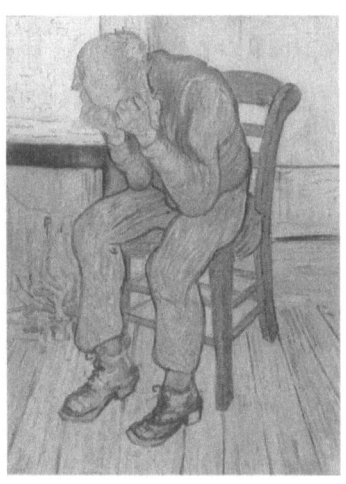

He also worked on interpretations of other artists' paintings, particularly the work of Millet, Gustave Courbet, and Jules Breton. Some of the work he produced includes studies of The Sower and Noonday Rest and variations on his own earlier work. His The Round of the Prisoners (1890,) was based on an engraving by Gustave Doré (1832–1883). It is possible that the face of the prisoner in the center of the painting looking towards the viewer is Van Gogh himself.

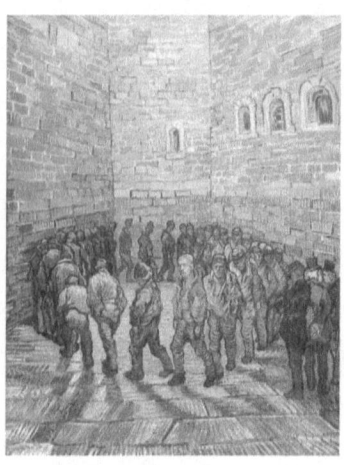

After this period of quite slow but steady improvement, Van Gogh suffered a severe relapse, including hallucination and delusions, as well as a complete inability to write between February and April 1890. He was severely depressed, but still able to paint and draw. As a rule, he created from memory, particularly what he described as "***reminiscences of the north***." One such example of these includes Two Peasant Women Digging in a Snow-Covered Field at Sunset (1890). This period was, according to Van Gogh, the only time his illness had any significant effect on his work, and his output, which was much diminished at this time.

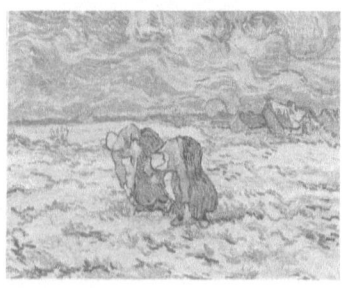

FIRST SIGNS OF APPRECIATION

❦

Symbolist poet Albert Aurier wrote a review of some of Van Gogh's work in the highly regarded Mercure de France journal in January of 1890, describing him as "*a genius*." More and more notoriety and honor began to come to Van Gogh, which struck him, and his circle as strange given his circumstances. He began to work on his five versions of L'Arlésienne in February 1890, taking as his model the charcoal sketch Gauguin produced and gave to Van Gogh during his stay in 1888. Also, that month, he received a singular honor to participate in the avantgarde society in Brussels called Les XX (Les Vingts).

❦

Les XX (Les Vingts). Henry de Groux (1866-1930), the Belgian Symbolist painter, made a drunken insult about Van Gogh's work during the opening dinner, and Toulouse-Lautrec, a longtime supporter of Van Gogh, demanded satisfaction, challenging Henry de Groux to a duel. Signac also stood behind Van Gogh and managed to get de Groux to apologize and leave the group.

Van Gogh had a showing at the Artistes Indépendants in Paris, and the noted Impressionist Claude Monet claimed that his work was the best in the show. Van Gogh was starting to achieve notoriety, despite his almost total inability to sell his paintings.

Van Gogh had heard about a doctor and amateur painter who had treated several other artists who had had emotional issues. Dr. Paul Gachet was recommended by Camille Pissarro, and so he moved to Auvers to be closer to him and his brother, leaving the clinic in May 1890. Interestingly, Van Gogh's first impression of Dr. Gachet was that he was "***more sick that I am.***"

But things were not going well in Van Gogh's mind. He created quite a lot during this period, including seventy completed oils in seventy days. These were mainly done from memory and were part of what he called his "***Memories of the North.***" In June, he painted several portraits of Dr. Gachet and completed the only etching of his career. His final completed work was a group of two paintings of the painter Charles Daubigny's Garden in July of 1890.

❦ X ❧
VAN GOGH'S DEATH

"I put my heart and my soul into my work and have lost my mind in the process."

— VINCENT VAN GOGH

※

Van Gogh wrote to his brother how he was absorbed in the sea of melancholy that was represented in the wheat fields that surrounded him.

> ". . knowing clearly what I wanted, I've painted another three large canvases since then. They're immense stretches of wheat fields under turbulent skies, and I made a point of trying to express sadness, extreme loneliness. You'll see this soon; I hope,,, for I hope to bring them to you in Paris as

> *soon as possible since I'd almost believe that these canvases will tell you what I can't say in words, what I consider healthy and fortifying about the countryside."*

❧

Still, Van Gogh's illness was continuing unabated, compounded by his worries about the future, since his brother had told him that he was considering leaving the Goupil & Company and striking out on his own. Then, on July 27th, 1890, Van Gogh shot himself in the chest with a 7mm Lefaucheux à broche revolver. He seems to have done this in a wheat field or a nearby barn, there were no witnesses, and he died the next day because the two doctors attending him could not remove the bullet, which caused an infection that killed him.

❧

His brother Theo, hearing of his situation, came to him and found him smoking in his room. He died in the early morning of July 29th. According to Theo, Vincent's final words were:

"The sadness will last forever."

❧

He was buried on July 30th in Auvers-sur-Oise, attended by many of the foremost painters of the day and Theo who died the next year and was buried beside him in 1914 after being exhumed from his original grave in Utrecht. His gravestone says only "***Ici repose Vincent van Gogh (1853-1890)***."

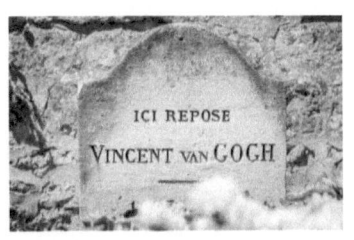

XI
POSTHUMOUS FAME AND REPUTATION

"If you hear a voice within you say 'you cannot paint,' then by all means paint, and that voice will be silenced."

— VINCENT VAN GOGH

※

Six weeks after Van Gogh's suicide, Theo Van Gogh organized a memorial exhibition of his brother's work. Theo was worried and ill and highly stressed out by the many sad things that had happened in the previous few weeks, and his health was deteriorating quickly. Shortly after the exhibition, he resigned from his job and suffered a severe nervous breakdown. He was admitted to an asylum with syphilis-related symptoms and died in January 1891.

❦

During his lifetime, Van Gogh was largely overlooked, although not totally written off, contributing works to several shows, but for whatever reason, he was often overlooked in favor of the more famous painters with whom he shared the stage. In 1887, he organized an exhibition in the Grand-Bouillon Restaurant du Chalet, 43 Avenue de Clichy, in Montmartre, including works by many of his friends, including Émile Bernard, Louis Anquetin, and Henri de Toulouse-Lautrec. All the other artists sold some of their work, but Van Gogh himself sold nothing.

❦

The Dutch painter Joseph Jacob Isaacson, a friend of Meyer de Haan and Theo van Gogh, wrote an article about Van Gogh in the 17 August 1889 issue of the Amsterdam weekly De Portefeuille. Van Gogh though was not honored by this recognition and wrote to Isaacson, asking him to stop writing about him. In 1889, Émile Bernard wrote a review of Van Gogh's work for Aurier's Moderniste, but when the journal folded, the article was shelved and only published in 1990.

❦

In January 1890 Albert Aurier wrote an enthusiastic essay called "***Les Isolés: Vincent van Gogh***" for the first issue refounding the Mercure de France. This article is credited with establishing Aurier as a leading art critic and beginning Van Gogh's rise to fame. Again, in March 1891, Octave Mirbeau wrote a review article in L'Echo de Paris about Van Gogh, to great acclaim. Later in 1891, Émile Bernard, a longtime friend of Van Gogh, wrote several short biographical sketches of Van Gogh for La Plume and Les Hommes d'aujourd'hui.

⁂

In German, Julius Meier-Graefe wrote several pieces about the work and life of Vincent Van Gogh, including his Entwicklungsgeschichte der modernen Kunst (Stuttgart, 1904 and later Munich 1927), "***Über Vincent van Gogh***," in the Sozialistische Monatshefte (February 1906), a book entitled Vincent van Gogh (Munich 1912), and another called Van Gogh der Zeichner (Van Gogh the Draftsman, published in Berlin in 1928 by Otto Wacker).

⁂

In England, the Bloomsbury group, closely associated with Cambridge University and King's College, London, became enamored of the narrative of the tortured artist, and Roger Fry wrote an essay called "***Vincent van Gogh***" in 1924. This article started the rumor that after he died, Van Gogh had disappeared until a 1910 show titled "***Post-Impressionist Exhibition***" in which

> *"his works dazzled, astonished and infuriated all cultured England"*

brought him back into the attention of the general public. He claimed that Van Gogh was

> *"the victim of the terrible intensity of his convictions - his conviction that somewhere one might lay hold of spiritual values compared with which all other values were of no account."*

Fry's essay described Van Gogh as "***a saint***" of art, describing his works as work that gave

> *"an expression in the paint for the desperate violence of his spiritual hunger...."*

This kind of adulation began a serious study of Van Gogh's work among English academics, at least from a biographical perspective. This same view was clearly held by the popular musician Don McLean when he wrote his song "***Vincent***" (1971), about Vincent Van Gogh, in which he tells the romantic but detailed and honest legend of the tortured artist.

❦

Starry, starry night, Paint your palette blue and gray
    Look out on a summer's day
    With eyes that know the darkness in my soul;
    Shadows on the hills Sketch the trees and the daffodils
    Catch the breeze and the winter chills
    In colors on the snowy linen land.

❦

Now I understand what you tried to say to me,
    And how you suffered for your sanity,
    How you tried to set them free,
    They would not listen, they did not know how
    Perhaps they'll listen now.

❦

Starry, starry night, Flaming flowers that brightly blaze

Swirling clouds in violet haze
Reflect in Vincent's eyes of china blue.

❦

Colors changing hue Morning fields of amber grain
    Weathered faces lined in pain
    Are soothed beneath the artist's loving hand.

❦

Now I understand what you tried to say to me
    And how you suffered for your sanity
    And how you tried to set them free
    They would not listen, they did not know how
    Perhaps they'll listen now.

❦

For they could not love you But still your love was true
    And when no hope was left inside On that starry, starry night
    You took your life as lovers often do
    But I could have told you, Vincent
    This world was never meant For one as beautiful as you.

❦

Starry, starry night Portraits hung in empty halls
    Frameless heads on nameless walls
    With eyes that watch the world and can't forget;
    Like the strangers that you've met The ragged men in ragged clothes
    A silver thorn, a bloody rose

Lie crushed and broken on the virgin snow.

❦

Now I think I know what you tried to say to me,
　　And how you suffered for your sanity,
　　And how you tried to set them free;
　　They would not listen, they're not listening still
　　Perhaps they never will....

❦

This song uses many of the paintings of Van Gogh to draw a portrait of a great but tortured artist and is profoundly moving.

❦

Clive Bell, another leading light of the Bloomsbury group, married to Virginia Woolf's sister, wrote his highly influential Art (1914), in which he included Van Gogh in the canon of great contemporary artists.

❦

As noted above, Van Gogh joined the "***Société des Artistes Indépendants***" in 1888, showing three of his paintings in their exhibition in Paris that year and two new paintings in 1889 at the Paris Exhibition, which was responsible for so many of now-popular items like the Eiffel Tower and the introduction of Balinese gamelan music that influenced the Impressionist composers of the time, and later convinced Gauguin to travel to Tahiti to paint the inhabitants of that tropical island.

※

In 1890 and 1891, the Société des Artistes Indépendants included ten of Van Gogh's paintings. In 1891, twelve of Van Gogh's drawings were shown by Les XX in Brussels. These exhibits made his work known to the then famous artists Claude Monet and Paul Signac.

※

In his last year of life, Van Gogh began at long last to receive the recognition he deserved. He was recognized as a great artist in France and Belgium, and shortly thereafter in the Netherlands, his homeland, and later in Germany.

JOHANNA VAN GOGH-BONGER

※

After his death, Theo Van Gogh's widow, Johanna Van Gogh-Bonger worked hard to promote the artist's work, using funds from the estate of her late husband to finance a series of exhibitions for Van Gogh's work. Following Theo's death, she moved to the Dutch town of Bussum with her son Vincent Willem, taking Vincent and Theo's art collection with her.

※

She remarried in 1901 to the painter Johan Cohen Gosschalk, and the family moved to Amsterdam two years later. At this point, she collected the letters of Van Gogh to his brother, with a few of Theo's letters that have survived, in 1914. In many ways, these exhibits and the letters established Van Gogh as the quintessential suffering artist, an exceedingly popular notion at the end of the Romantic period.

During the First World War, Van Gogh became recognized as the greatest contemporary artist in German and Austria, and shortly thereafter, in Switzerland. Interestingly, because of the severe economic depression that engulfed the German-speaking countries, following World War I, the collections of Van Gogh's works were largely dissolved and sold to American and English collectors, bringing him fame and notoriety in English-speaking countries in the 1920s. American novelist Irving Stone wrote a biography of Vincent Van Gogh in 1934, called Lust for Life, based mostly on the letters that were published in 1914. A movie, also called Lust for Life, was made in 1956, directed by renowned Italian director Vincente Minnelli, the husband of Judy Garland and father to Liza Minnelli. This film was also based on the book, further adding to the mystery of Van Gogh's name.

THE VAN GOGH MUSEUM

※

Following Johanna's death in 1925, the Van Gogh art collection passed to her son, the engineer Vincent Willem Van Gogh, who lent his uncle's paintings to the Stedelijk Museum in Amsterdam in 1930.

※

As Van Gogh's fame grew, though, there were calls for the creation of a dedicated museum for his work. And so, finally, in 1962, with the help and consent of the State of the Netherlands, Vincent Willem Van Gogh placed the Van Gogh collection with the Vincent Van Gogh Foundation. In return, the Netherlands agreed to build the Van Gogh Museum and subsequently to ensure that the collection is accessible to everyone forever.

※

Eleven years later, in 1974, the works were moved from the Stedelijk Museum to a specially designed building by Gerrit Rietveld.

❦

Queen Juliana of the Netherlands opened the Van Gogh Museum in Amsterdam in 1973. Since then, it has drawn visitors from every corner of the world. According to their website, two million people now visit the museum each year.

> *"I can do nothing about it if my paintings don't sell. The day will come, though, when people will see that they're worth more than the cost of the paint and my subsistence, very meager in fact, that we put into them."*

❦

On October 28, 1888, Van Gogh wrote these prophetic words to his brother. Almost a century later, they became true.

❦

There began to be a great deal of interest in the work and life of Van Gogh in the twentieth century, including a work by French playwright, Antonin Artaud, called Van Gogh le suicidé de la société (1947), Paul Celan mentions Van Gogh's ear in his poem "***Mächte, Gewalten***" (Powers, Dominions). Dutch novelist Theun de Vries wrote a novel, Vincent in Den Haag (Vincent in The Hague), which takes place between 1881 and 1883, and American Charles Bukowski wrote a poem on Van Gogh called "***Working Out***." There are numerous other references to the great painter, who has since become something of a cultural icon.

※

The first major exhibition from Van Gogh's estate was in 1892 in the Amsterdam "***Panorama***" Building.

※

In 1893, Julien Leclercq brought together an exhibition that included Van Gogh, Gauguin, and other artists he defined as "***Modernists***," and toured this exhibition through Scandinavia, ending in Berlin. In Paris, there were two retrospective exhibitions of Van Gogh's work in 1895 and 1896 mounted by Ambroise Vollard in his galleries. In 1901, Leclercq organized another Parisian show he named The Van Gogh Exhibition at the Galerie Bernheim-Jeune, which greatly increased the artist's fame.

※

His work was embraced by the Berlin Secessionists in 1901, particularly championed by the art dealers Bruno Cassirer and Paul Cassirer. In late December 1901 until January 1902, Paul Cassirer organized a solo exhibition of Van Gogh's work in Berlin for the first time. Then in 1908, Paul Cassirer arranged another exposition in Berlin, which included the painting Peach Blossoms in the Crau on loan from Anna Boch.

※

Ironically, considering the artist's aversion to the commodification of art, Paul Cassirer was the man who established a lucrative market for Van Gogh's work, and then with the help of Johanne Van Gogh-Bonger, managed to control the market prices. In 1906 Bruno Cassirer published a small volume of selected letters, translated into German.

※

Johanna also contributed important works to Roger Fry's 1910 London exhibition, and to the Sonderbund exhibition of 1912 in Cologne. This was organized by an independent committee of artists, collectors, and museum professionals, with on loans from Cassirer and other art dealers.

※

Another retrospective show was staged in 1905 in the Stedelijk Museum Amsterdam, followed by a display in 1914, concentrating on Van Gogh's drawings.

❧ XII ❧
WHY ARE VAN GOGH'S PAINTINGS SO VALUABLE?

"Paintings have a life of their own that derives from the painter's soul."

— VINCENT VAN GOGH

※

In Van Gogh's lifetime, he sold a total of one painting. It was during the Les XX exposition in 1890 that he sold The Red Vineyard, bought by Anna Boch, an Impressionist painter and heiress to a ceramics fortune, for four hundred francs. She was also the sister of Eugene Boch.

※

After he died, however, various museums purchased works by Van Gogh, including the Folkwang Museum in Hagen, a gallery run by Karl-Ernst Osthaus. Similarly, in the 1930s, the Museum of Modern Art in New York City bought many of his works as did the Tate Gallery in London, taking advantage of the severe depression in Germany, where many of his works had gravitated after his death.

※

Johanna Van Gogh-Bonger, the mother of a newborn baby named Vincent and recent widow of Theo, was the most important person in the posthumous fame of Vincent Van Gogh. Theo's greatest legacy was the collection of his brother's artworks, and as a widow, she felt the need to get the most out of this inheritance. As a member of a prominent artistic family from Amsterdam, Johanna was well connected in the European art community, and she used these connections to increase the value of her inheritance through shows, publications, and other publicity. Rather than selling off his work one by one, she strove instead to make his work widely known and thus was able to amass a small fortune from the sale of a few of his works but mainly from loaning significant works to major galleries.

※

Van Gogh, although he was unable to sell much of his work, was known and admired in the circle of highly influential Impressionist and post-Impressionist artists in France, Belgium, and the Netherlands. Thus, when Johanna Van Gogh-Bongers began her work, the fact that she was a woman worked, in some ways, to her advantage. People did not expect her to be an astute businesswoman. She managed to maintain an almost complete collection of Van Gogh's work until 1906.

※

The reasons for the high value of Van Gogh's artwork stem from many different things, including the difficulty he had in selling his work during his life, as well as the dogged commitment of Johanna Van Gogh-Bongers in maintaining the legend of the starving artist, troubled with insanity and substance abuse. This idea, as well as the idea of the artist who only became known after his death, is a convenient myth for many who view art as a comfortable place to invest their fortunes. His collection is not going to grow since he is dead. Similarly, his work defies characterization as any particular style, although it is similar to the Impressionists, and various other styles popular in the 1880s. He had a short but remarkably prolific career, and many of his works have been forged. There are many elements to the story that are compelling, but the work of the artist has an integrity of its own as well, and it holds up well in the modern world.

※

As an example of the astronomical amounts paid for his work in recent years, His Portrait of Dr. Gachet, from 1890, sold in 1990 for $137,700,000.00; the Portrait of Joseph Roulin (the Postmaster) sold for what would be $103,800.000.00 in 1989; Portrait of the Artist Without a Beard sold for $101,000,000.00 in 1998; Irises, for $100,000,000.00; A Wheatfield with Cypresses for $87,900,000.00; The Wheat fields for $81,300,00.00 in 2017. This is only a partial (and constantly changing) list of the many works of Van Gogh that have sold for huge amounts. The common denominator in all these sales is the disconnection from the work's significance, quality, or skill required to make it. What does not change is the value of the name Van Gogh as a cultural touchstone.

And thus, ironically, the artist who eschewed monetization of his work survived in the cultural memory as a name, a label of great value to those who collect and commodify art. The only other artists who come close to Van Gogh as a valuable label are Pablo Picasso and Andy Warhol, both of whom were very wealthy men at their deaths.

❧ XIII ☙
HOW CAN WE USE THE LIFE OF VAN GOGH IN OUR OWN LIVES?

※

The story of Van Gogh is the story of many misunderstood artists. His extreme poverty and his misery, and the misery he gave to others in his life because he sacrificed so much are important things to know about modern life. While we tend to lionize heroes today, military figures, musicians, politicians, and the like, the artist who stays true to his vision is rare and difficult to detect. In fact, most of the books written about Vincent Van Gogh is romanticized and in at least some ways presumptuous. The fact of the matter is, with art, it is difficult to know what a painter intended other than the actual work itself. It is worth learning this lesson when reading about great artists because the fact is, nobody knows exactly what the ineffable quality that makes art artist stand out from the others. It is a mystery and one that is continuously changing. Art is not a commodity, despite its value, because there is no inherent value to art, other than what one person feels. It has value because we imbue it with value. There is nothing in particular that makes one work valuable or great; but when one looks at a great work of art, one is determined to find that thing that makes it better than all other art. And it is undiscoverable. Vincent Van Gogh suffered because he sought that quality all his life and finally, perhaps, found it in a few of his paintings. I would be willing to be that he would not agree with all the millionaires who paid so much money for his art, though. I would be willing to bet that his most personal works, the Sien collection, is what he valued the most because here is where he had a chance at real happiness, and it was taken from him by judgmental people too worried about what others thought than his happiness. This may be the truest tragedy in the life of Van Gogh that he had a chance of happiness, and it was snatched from him. Perhaps we will never know.

✤ XIV ✤
FURTHER READING

❧❧❧

- Naifeh, Steven, and White-Smith, Gregory, Van Gogh: The Life, New York: Random House, 2011
- Suh, Anna H., Vincent Van Gogh: A Self-Portrait in Art and Letters, New York: Black Dog & Leventhal Publishers: Distributed by Workman Pub. Co., c2006.
- Walther, Ingo F.(ed.), and Metzger, Rainer, Van Gogh: The Complete Paintings, 2 volumes, Köln: Benedikt Taschen, 1993

Copyright © 2018 by Kolme Korkeudet Oy

All rights reserved.

No part of this book may be reproduced in any form or by any electronic or mechanical means, including information storage and retrieval systems, without written permission from the author, except for the use of brief quotations in a book review.

YOUR FREE EBOOK!

As a way of saying thank you for reading our book, we're offering you a free copy of the below eBook.

Happy Reading!

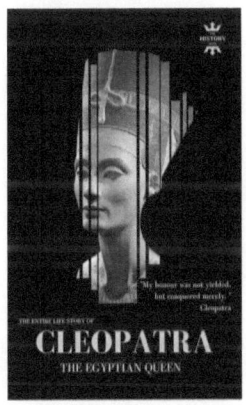

GO WWW.THEHISTORYHOUR.COM/CLEO/

www.ingramcontent.com/pod-product-compliance
Lightning Source LLC
Chambersburg PA
CBHW031447210526
45464CB00005B/2358

9781728919058